Can you Try?

COLOURING BOOK

Challenging Colouring book for you with awesome mandala style patterns

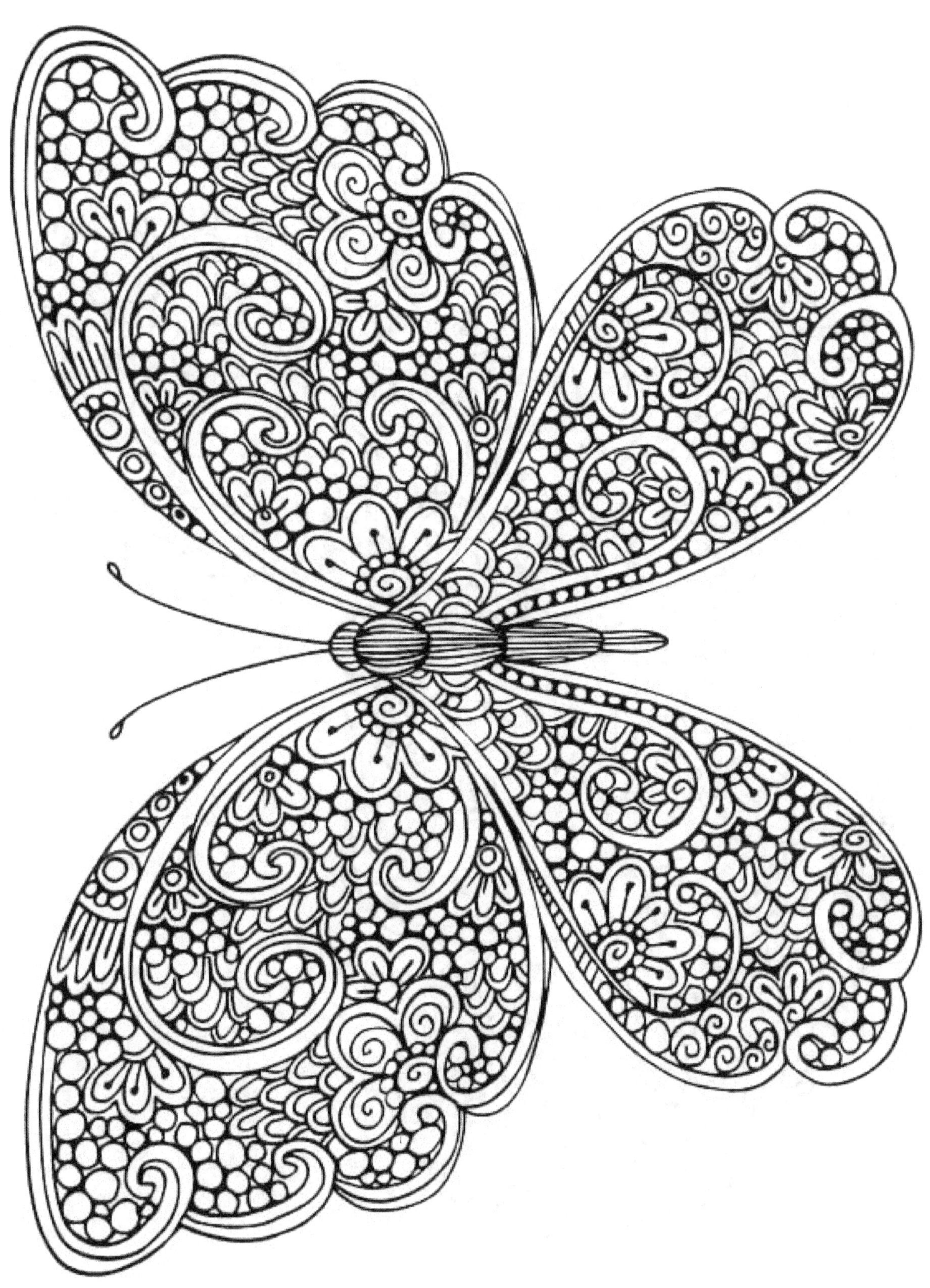

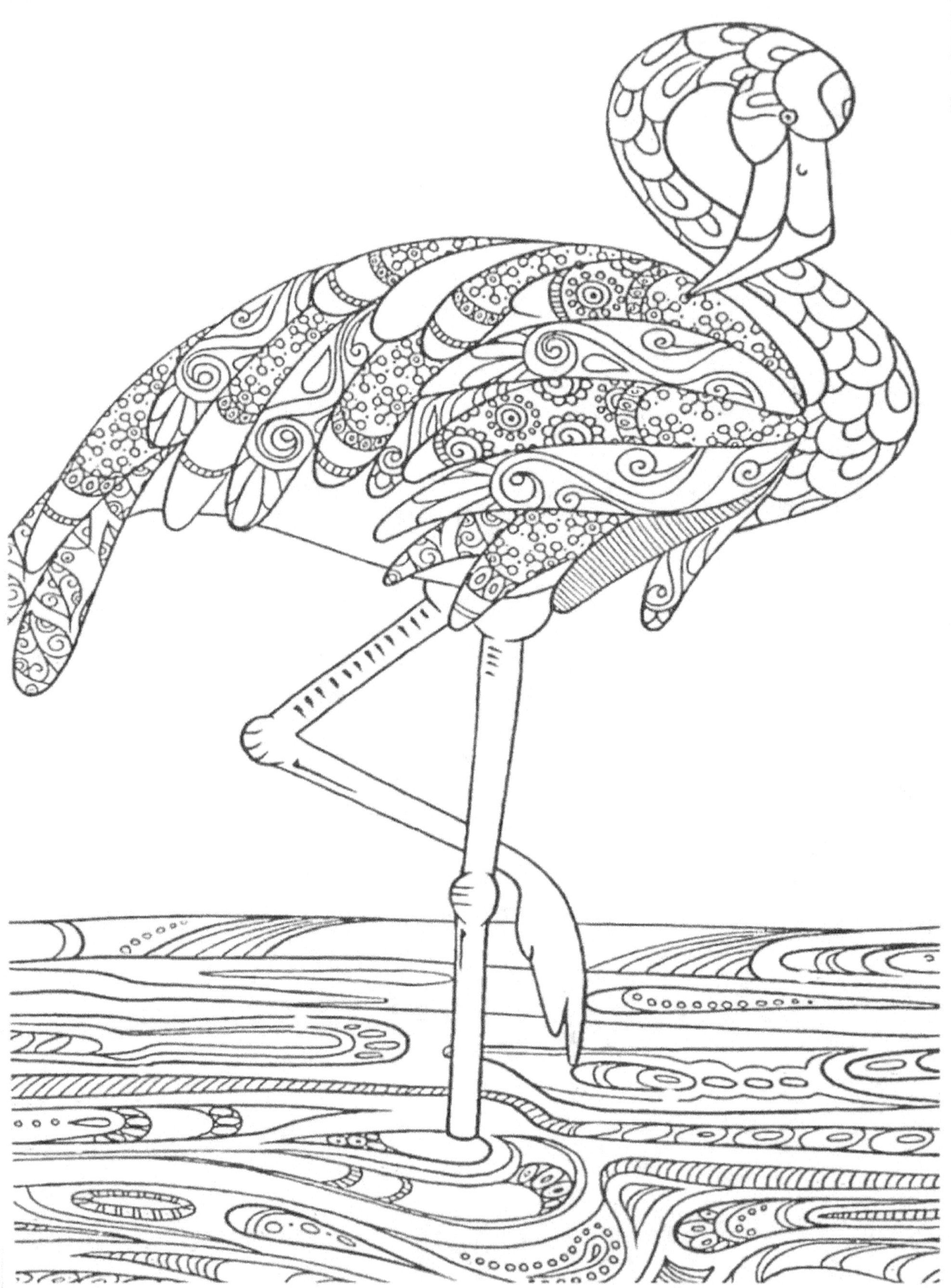

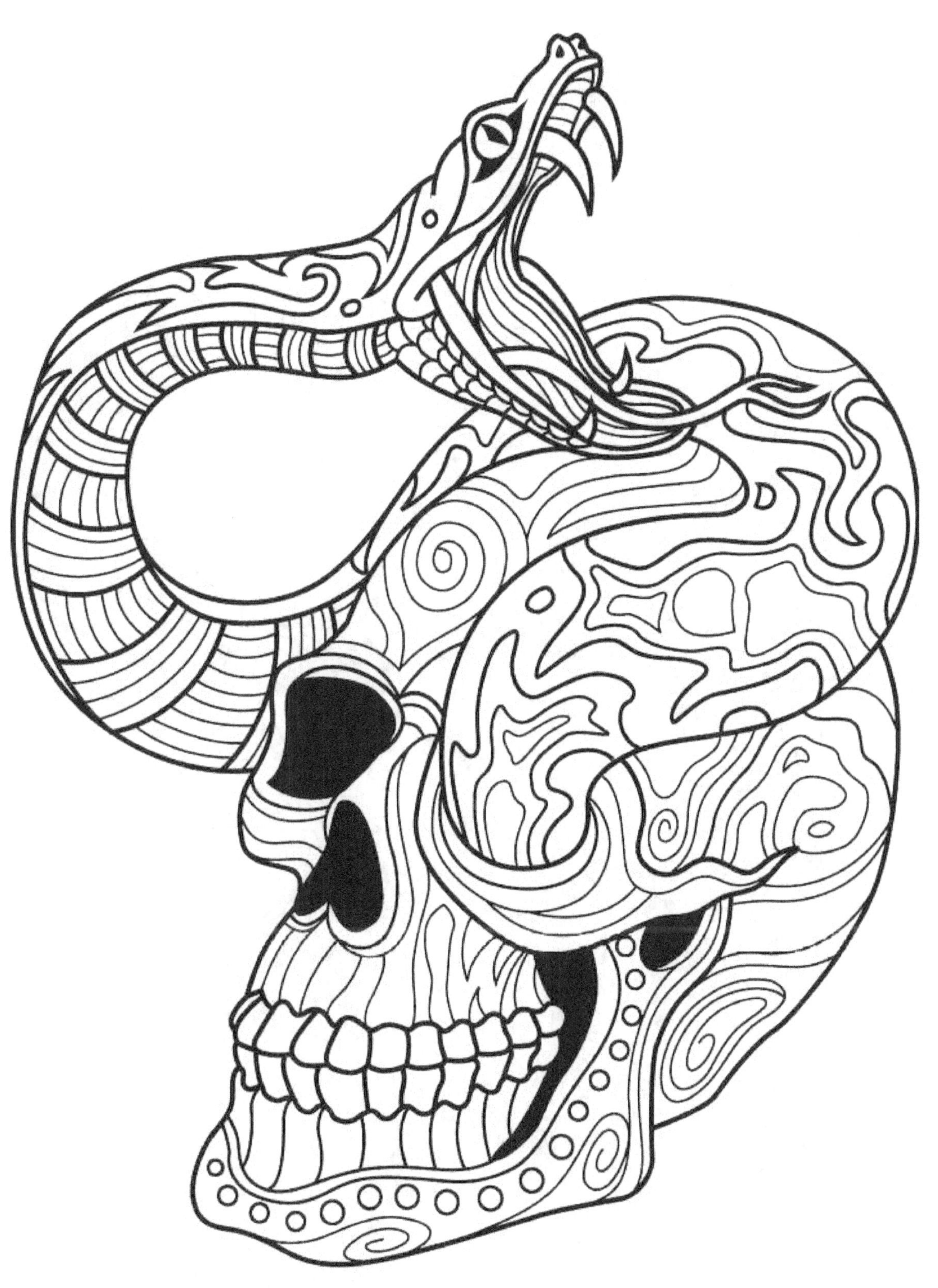

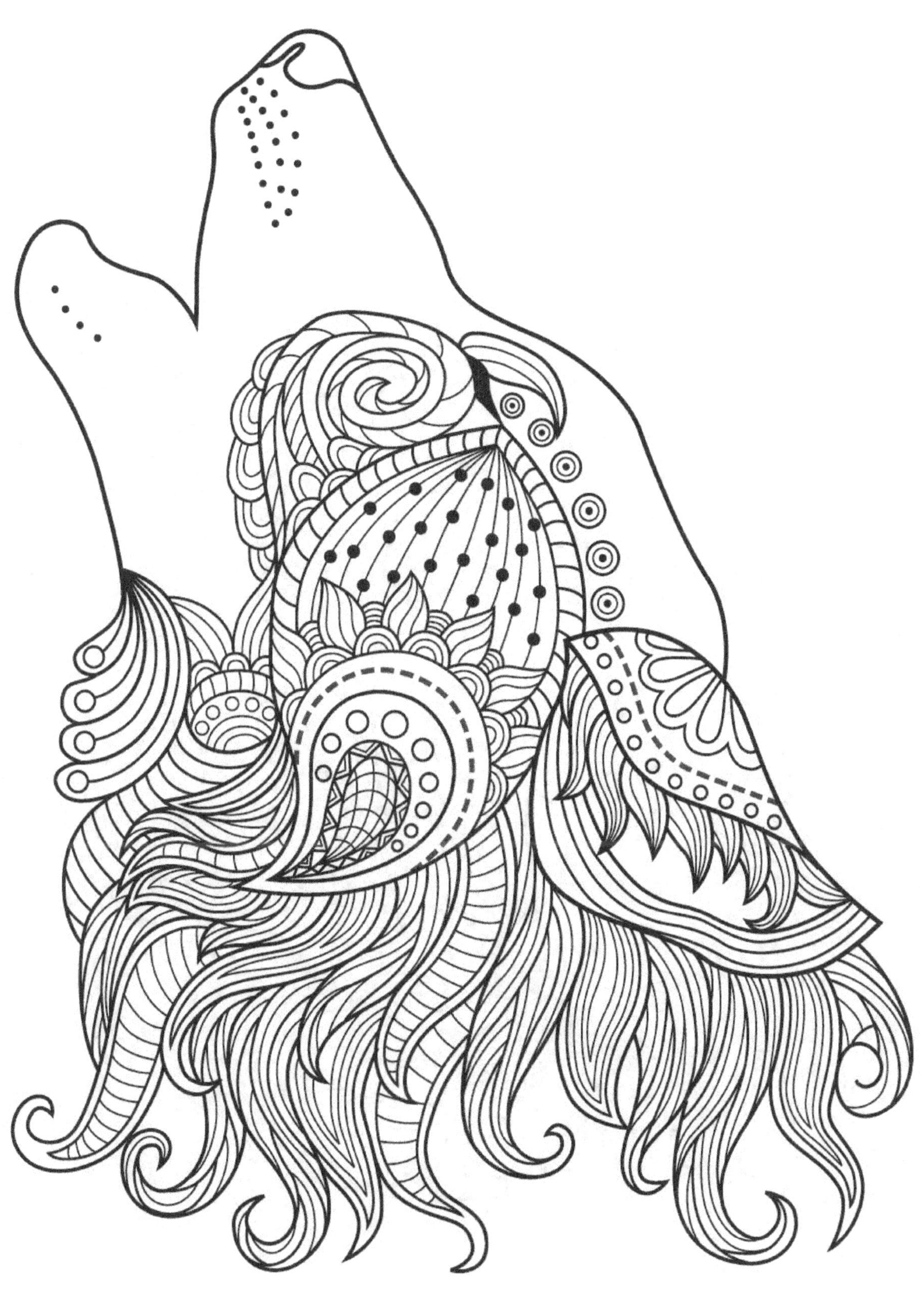

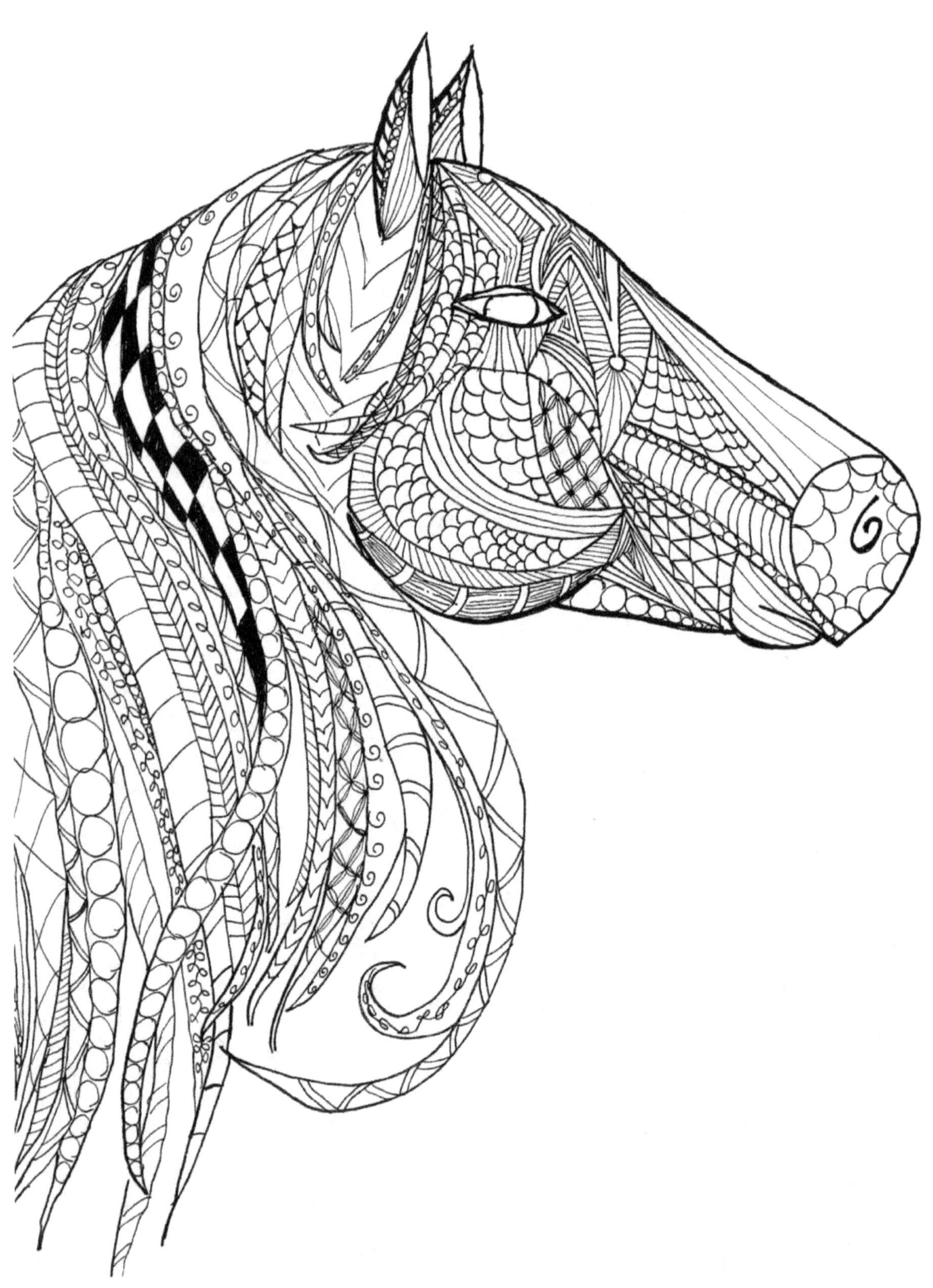

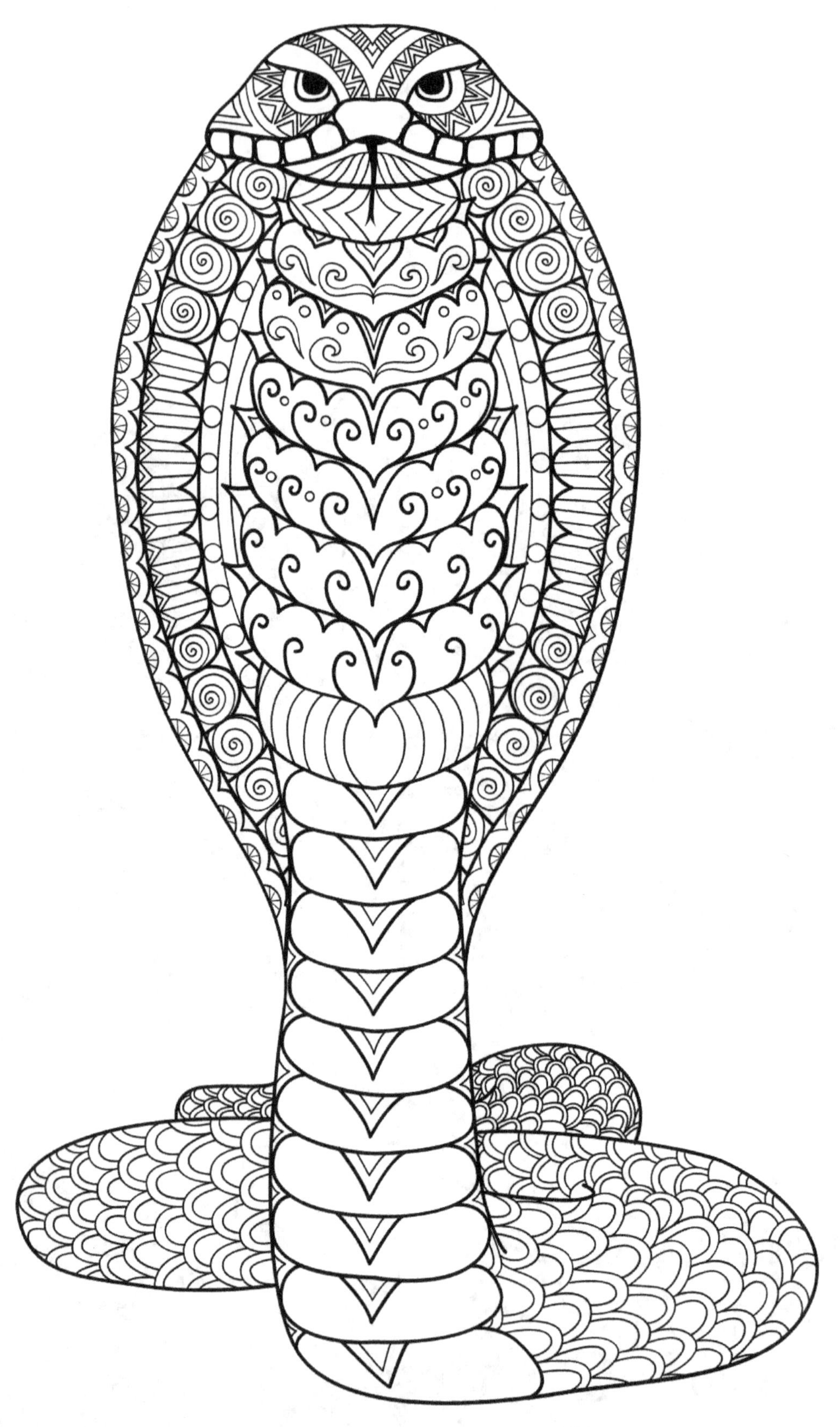